M000218245

# Lost in Yesterday

---

*Commemorating the 70th Anniversary of*
*Margaret Mitchell's*
*Gone with the Wind*

---

# Lost in Yesterday

*Peter Bonner*

## Peter Bonner

*firstWorks Publishing / Marietta GA*

# Lost in Yesterday
## All Rights Reserved Copyright © 2006
### Peter Bonner

All rights reserved. No part of this book may be reproduced or transmitted in any form or by any means, graphic, electronic, or mechanical, including photocopying, recording, taping, or by any information storage or retrieval system, without the permission in writing from the Publisher.

The book is not intended to reprint all of the information available to the author or publisher on the subject, but rather to simplify, complement and supplement other available sources. The reader is encouraged to read all available material and to learn as much as possible about the subject. Some of these materials are listed under SUGGESTED READING elsewhere in this book.

For Information, please address:

FirstWorks Publishing Co., Inc.
P.O. Box 93 / Marietta, GA 30061-0093
Email: firstworks@mindspring.com

Cover Design by Audra Pettyjohn, Graphic Artist
Evolution Designs, Dawsonville, GA

Library of Congress Control Number 2006921244

ISBN: 0-9716158-9-6
ISBN: 978-0-9716158-9-2

Printed in the United States of America

One of the most entertaining and informative books I have read in recent memory is *Lost in Yesterday* by Peter Bonner. He can resuscitate all those yesteryears and make them live again within its pages.

My abiding interest in his recall is the lasting resonance of rich detail which he conveys, so much of this, my wife, Terry Lynn, and I have personally experienced from his many visits with us.

We dwell in an historic residence on a site in Georgia, in close proximity to those places referred to by Peter Bonner with his tongue-in-cheek humor.

It was my privilege to have spoken the opening lines in the movie "Gone With The Wind" as Brent Tarleton, and offer my gratitude to the diminutive giant that Margaret Mitchell still is to this very day.

Bonner's scholarly research evokes bittersweet memories, and recaptures both the sorrow and nobility of that tragic era of heroes and grace, and I highly recommend this as a must-read for anyone with an abiding interest in those captivating times.

Fred Crane / "Brent Tarleton

To attempt to say "thank you" to ALL of my friends and family who have supported me throughout this endeavor, or given me insight into another of Margaret Mitchell's stories along the way, would be a daunting task. But with my hat in my hand and my head slightly bowed, I humbly say *thank you.*

To my wife, Sharon, who encouraged me and typed for me, I couldn't have done it without you. Historical & Hysterical Tours was your creative genius and I am reminded of that every time someone reads my business card and laughs. I love you.

Now to Him who *"commended His love toward me in that while I was yet a sinner, sent Christ to die for me."* (Romans 5:8), I dedicate this book.

*A Native Son's Dedication to Margaret Mitchell
In commemoration of the 70th Anniversary
of the 1936 literary release of
"Gone With the Wind"*

As a Civil War historian, I hold vouchsafe
Margaret Mitchell's dedication to writing about an era that will
forever intrigue her readers;
her devotion to accuracy of a time that--despite her
remarkable research and tenor of presentation--
continues to be misunderstood.

As a native son of Clayton County,
I hold dear the Irish will and determination of
Margaret Mitchell's ancestors who lived, toiled, and died
for the way of life of a people caught up in the
evolutionary cultural transition of the times.

Margaret Mitchell understood the heritage of her people
who were committed to survival--despite a Civil War, despite
the
horrors and deprivations of war-- and,
who, seeing their world disintegrate before their eyes,
could only rely on their own self-sufficiency to survive.

Margaret Mitchell's *Gone With the Wind*
is more than a love story...
it is the living history of a Nation's people
pitted against each other--Free Men and Slave--
brought together because of commerce;
yet challenged by the Deity to love one another.

## A Word From The Author

I love to tell stories. And, I have a few to tell...

It begins with one of my ancestors who, upon his return from fighting in the *War Between the States* (as we Southerners prefer to call the Civil War), traded his cavalry horse for the Bonner homeplace.

My family history and all I learned about the old dwelling and its connection with the Civil War intrigued me. At nearly every family event, aunts and uncles would tell stories about my ancestors, but the seriousness of my interest in Civil War history really began when I was in seventh grade.

I credit my parents with motivating me in my love of history and instilling in me an appreciation of the past and respecting all that my ancestors had done. You know, they set my soul afire!

Now, as a father myself, I think back to all those countless hours listening to family lore and, in the reality of it all, there is a very simple truth: no one is perfect; life is not perfect--and life is what we make of it.

Family and friends have told me that I inherited some of my mother's great storytelling ability, but my father is fond of saying, "I don't know where Peter got his storytelling from." And then, my father launches into a story of his own(!)

My seventh grade history teacher encouraged me to write our family stories and motivated me to delve deeper into

Civil War history. Of course, I played the usual games most boys do; and having owned guns since I was ten years old, went hunting with my Dad on our farm.

My college years began at Clayton State in Morrow, Georgia and then I transferred to Criswell College in Dallas, Texas where I received a Bachelor of Arts degree. Over the years, my growing affinity for research and for storytelling produced some really *quirky* and anecdotal yarns that have given me a confidence, resulting in a somewhat "dramatic" flair to my historical presentations (sometimes hysterical). I dress in period costume which also enhances my war stories and tales of old Jonesboro.

In the interest of research, I participated in battle re-enactments as a member of the 30th Georgia Company E that marched off to war from Jonesboro in 1861, and which returned to fight the Battle of Jonesboro in 1864. My commitment to historical accuracy was furthered by my participation in the battles of Chickamauga, Kennesaw Mountain, Tunnel Hill, Resaca, and the battle of Browns Mill, all which occurred in Georgia.

Another activity I am deeply committed to is teaching students. Over the last fifteen years, I have had the good fortune to be invited into schools to present history and storytelling programs to first through eighth graders. The children enjoy my interactive teaching approach that gives them a "hands-on" learning experience. They have the opportunity to not only touch the artifacts from another era, but also to wear some of the clothing from that period.

It's almost a given that children will ask me if I fought in the Civil War(!) It not only makes me proud that they've been caught up in the history I bring them, as many teachers have told me, but that their short excursion back in time inspires them to want to know more.

One of my true loves is my *Gone With The Wind Tour* that began fifteen years ago at the Confederate Civil War

Cemetery in Jonesboro. I dressed in Confederate garb and told the tales of Union and Confederate soldiers who fought and died in the Battle of Jonesboro. In a manner of speaking, I was *lost in yesterday*, but I must dedicate the rest of this story to Margaret Mitchell...

Folks who took my tour began sending me copies of letters from their ancestors who fought in the Civil War, both for the North and for the South. My research escalated and I began uncovering some startling coincidences with Margaret Mitchell's GWTW. I had always heard that Miss Mitchell described her book as fiction and that it was not based upon any true stories. However, she wrote a letter to Dr. Mark Allen Patton of Virden, Illinois, dated July 11, 1936, and said, *"Practically all the incidences in the book are true. Of course, they didn't all happen to the same person, and a few of them didn't happen in Atlanta."* Margaret Mitchell's "Gone With The Wind" Letters 1936-1949, Stephens Mitchell/MacMillan/1976,

I interpreted that to mean that her book was not entirely fiction and that *maybe* some of the old folklore of Jonesboro and the Fitzgerald family (Margaret Mitchell's great-grandparents) had more validity than previously believed. As my touring guests quoted the many passages from GWTW, and swooned and fantasized about the book and the characters Margaret Mitchell had brought to life, I seemed to be propelled to the next level. I began writing down the many anecdotes the locals of Jonesboro had told me and began including these stories in my tour for the thousands of visitors who came looking for *Tara* and Margaret Mitchell's timeless characters.

I've been a lifelong resident of Clayton County, Georgia. (For those of you who aren't familiar with the Atlanta area, it's about twenty miles south of Atlanta by way of the old Jonesboro Road or, *the road to Tara*.) Throughout my research of Clayton County and Jonesboro, in particular, I learned that Jonesboro had played a more significant role during the Battle of Atlanta than most people realize.

In a theoretical vein, I believe that Margaret Mitchell wrote her novel as her dedication to that War, rather than *using* it as the backdrop for her love story. She wrote: *"...Somehow the period of the Sixties always seemed much more real to me than my own era."* *Letter to Miss Harriet Ross Colquitt, Bluffton, South Carolina, August 7, 1936//Margaret Mitchell's Gone With The Wind" Letters, 1936-1949; Stephens Mitchell, McMillan Co. 1975*

I believe that Margaret Mitchell's family taught her not so much of love, as of survival. I'm also inclined to believe that the ferocity of her Irish heritage was a subliminal character in her book. Yet, all that she was told about the War Between the States must have left the most indelible of impressions. After all, she recalled sitting upon the laps of several of her great-aunts and uncles listening to their accounts of the battles and the way it was in little Jonesboro during the War Between the States.

There has been an abundance (and a redundancy) of many facts related to Margaret Mitchell's ancestors; specifically, her great-grandparents, grandmother, and her own mother who may (or may not) have been incorporated within the pages of GWTW.

However, there remains little "new" information. What has been available to one has been available to all about Margaret Mitchell, about her family, as well as the ancestral anecdotes within the archives in Georgia, the historical societies, the Margaret Mitchell House, Margaret Mitchell's own letters, and county records.

What lies between the pages of books written *about* Margaret Mitchell and her writing of GWTW is, in my opinion, subject to interpretation. I have endeavored to present the facts as stated in documents and those anecdotal stories learned through research, as well as those personally recounted to me, and let my readers form their own conclusions...

In 1937, a little drugstore in Fayetteville served as the meeting place where a group of ladies gathered to discuss their plans for a library. Included in one of their meetings was talk about the new hit novel, *Gone With The Wind*.

Unbeknownst to the ladies, Ms. Mitchell overheard their conversation about her book and their anxiousness to raise funds to purchase a little house that would become Fayetteville's first library.

Margaret Mitchell walked over to the ladies and introduced herself as the author of the book. During the course of the conversation, Ms. Mitchell commented on their ambitious project and that she admired their determination to assume the task of establishing a library.

Over the years, Ms. Mitchell was their quiet benefactor, and when they had amassed the funds they needed, they purchased the little house that sat within view of the Fayetteville Cemetery.

Sometime during the 1940s, the ladies asked Ms. Mitchell if they could name the library in her honor. Appreciative and humbled, she consented. Thus started the Margaret Mitchell Memorial Library in Fayetteville.

On August 1, 1949, a day filled with a pounding rain, Margaret Mitchell pulled into the parking lot of the library she had helped fund into existence, stepped out, and opened the trunk of her car. She had brought down to the ladies another delivery of books.

From the back door of the little repository, she might have glanced across to the cemetery that was the resting place of her Fitzgerald ancestors, and of her cousins, the Holliday's. It would be her last trip to the land she knew and loved so well.

Two weeks later, on August 11, 1949, Margaret Mitchell and her husband, John Marsh, parked their car along Peachtree Street, just beyond 13th Street, bound for a night at the theater. A taxi driver came speeding down Peachtree, unable to stop, skidding out of control and striking Ms. Mitchell. The cabbie was charged with driving while intoxicated and convicted of involuntary manslaughter.

Margaret "Peggy" Mitchell lay in a coma in Grady Hospital for five days. At 11:59 a.m. on August 16, 1949, Margaret Mitchell joined her fellow literary immortals...

In 1968, Jonesboro received its corporate charter to become Historical Jonesboro, Inc. As such, its nonprofit status would assure the history and heritage of Clayton County. Its chairperson, Mrs. Margery Middlebrooks-Butler, diligently worked to accomplish this and was quoted in the June 20, 1986 *Gone With The Wind Supplement* of the Clayton News-Daily:

> *"During forty years of happy and productive business civic associations, it became my burning desire to help Jonesboro and Clayton County achieve its rightful recognition as the locale of the turning point of the Battle of Atlanta during the 'War Between The States,' also to clean up, beautify, and to save the county's heritage by having the distinction of being the worlds' renown home of Gone With The Wind."*

Also pictured at the ribbon-cutting ceremony in Jonesboro is Margaret Mitchell's brother, Stephens Mitchell. The following year, Stephens Mitchell was named to the Board of Directors of Historical Jonesboro, Inc. Mrs. Margery Middlebrooks-Butler accomplished what she set out to do and obtained Stephens Mitchell's declaration that Clayton County was to be the *official* home of *Gone With The Wind*.

·P·A·R·T· ·O·N·E·

# 22 Peter Bonner

# A Little History

*Atlanta* began not as "Atlanta" but as *Terminus* in 1837. The Western & Atlantic Railroad joined middle and north Georgia at the completion--or *terminus*--of the rail lines. Today, the historical area known as Underground Atlanta has a marker designating the actual location of the tracks.

In 1842, with only six buildings and thirty inhabitants, Terminus was renamed Marthasville, as a tribute to Governor Lumpkin, whose daughter's name was Martha Atalanta. In 1845, the name *Atlanta* was proposed by Mr. Edgar Thompson of the Western & Atlantic Railroad which was under the Georgia rail system. In 1847, the name Marthasville was changed and the town was officially incorporated as *Atlanta*. At that time, Governor Lumpkin stated the name change was due to his political enemies and "the low voice of envy."

The Creek Indians ceded a large portion of their tribal lands to the State of Georgia under the Treaty of Indian Springs in 1821. In 1823, Leakesville (Jonesboro) was founded and chartered as part of Fayette County.

According to City of Jonesboro records, the Monroe Railroad and Banking Company of Macon, Georgia ordered a survey of the land from Macon to a point just below the Chattahoochee River and what would become the city of Atlanta. The tracks reached Leaksville in 1843; however, a financial depression began that same year delaying construction and causing the Monroe Railroad to fall into bankruptcy.

In 1845, the Macon and Western Railroad Company was organized and the railroad was completed with continuous rail service from Macon to the town that would be known as *Atlanta.*

Colonel Samuel Goode Jones, the civil engineer who planned the Leaksville portion of the railroad, had an interest in the future growth of Leaksville. With his engineering expertise, he mapped out the streets in the village and assigned numbers to sections and lots. In appreciation for all that Colonel Jones had done, the local citizenry changed the town's name to *Jonesboro.* That was in 1845. Incorporation followed in 1859, two years before the War Between the States.

While Colonel Jones contributed much to the little town, his son, Thomas, was a student at V.M.I. (Virginia Military Institute), and had the good fortune to study under Thomas "Stonewall" Jackson. Thomas Jones was commissioned into the Confederate Army and was present at the surrender of Lee's Army at Appomattox Courthouse in Virginia. Northern General Joshua Lawrence Chamberlain wrote that he met young Jones under a flag of truce as the surrender was being negotiated. (Young Jones later received a law degree, served as a judge, and Governor of Alabama.)

Because of the railroad, Jonesboro became a commercial center serving Fayette and Henry Counties, as well as Clayton. On market days, its streets and loading docks were the scene of considerable activity, and during autumn, bales of cotton lined the railroad beside the depot waiting shipment to other points. In addition to the several larger and imposing private residences in town, there were farms and plantations which formed the backbone of the local economy. City of Jonesboro History

Atlanta was the "hub" of the South, as it remains today. In 1861, three major rail lines served Atlanta which supplied the Confederacy with troop deployments, munitions, and supplies.

In the summer of 1863, riots broke out in New York. The passage of a conscription bill and the subsequent selection of its first draftees triggered the week-long chaos. Youth's History of the Great Civil War in the U..S.1861-1865, R.G. Horton; Vanevri-Horton & Co. 1867. New York's Irish population thought the freed slaves would go North and take their jobs. And, one familiar call throughout the North was: *"We do not want to keep sending men to die!"* Many accused Lincoln of not having an *"exit strategy."*

I have a letter written by an Ohio soldier who stated: *"I wish Ohio would secede!"*

Indeed, the war was not going well for Lincoln. His military leaders were continually challenged by Southern commanders whose field tactics resulted in heavy losses for the Federals.

After three long and bloody years of war, Lincoln's generals had failed to bring the war to the South. He called General Ulysses S. Grant to Washington for a meeting in March 1864. Later that month, Grant met with W.T. Sherman in Nashville to convey the war strategies discussed with Lincoln.

In May, General Robert E. Lee served up yet another defeat for the Federals, successfully halting Grant's battle campaign to capture Richmond; nearly 140,000 Federal troops gave up 65,000 of their comrades.

Close to losing the war and probably re-election, Lincoln's

future was tenuous at best. His re-election campaign was not going well. The political cartoonists of the day took to portraying him as an ape. And then, there was General George B. McClellan ("Little Mac")--who Lincoln had fired in 1862-- and who now was his Democrat rival. McClellan was running on a platform of negotiating peace with the South, and was quoted as saying,. *"Let 'em go... Let them start their own country."*

With Grant failing to capture Richmond, Lincoln was convinced that if the South--Atlanta, in particular--was not captured, victory would never be his--and he would not be re-elected. The outcome of the War rested entirely with General William T. Sherman to *"take Georgia"* and destroy Atlanta in what would become known as the *Atlanta Campaign.*

Atlanta was *the* challenge--and *the prize.* It was the South's principal depot with a railroad network that reached throughout the Confederacy supplying Lee's armies with arms and munitions--Atlanta had to be captured.

## The Atlanta Campaign
## May - September 1864

The Union Army of the Cumberland was commanded by General George Thomas; the Army of the Tennessee by General James B. McPherson; and the Army of the Ohio by General John M. Schofield. All three were directly answerable to Sherman who commanded their nearly 100,000 forces.

Awaiting "Uncle Billy" Sherman (as his men affectionately called him) were three corps of 50,000 troops under the command of Confederate General Joseph E. Johnston and his Generals William J. Hardee, John B. Hood, and Leonidas Polk. It is estimated that an additional 15,000 men reinforced the Confederate ranks, bringing their forces to approximately 65,000.

The Atlanta Campaign began in earnest in May. Skirmishes and battles between Federal and Confederate troops were fought from Ringgold, Georgia, south through Tunnel Hill, Rocky Face, and the two bloody battles at Resaca, where approximately 2,750 Yankee casualties and 2,800 Rebel losses occurred.

Johnston--fearing heavy casualties and knowing that he could not hold Resaca against Sherman's advancing troops--sent orders to destroy the telegraph lines and burn the railroad bridge at Resaca, severely interrupting the North's flow of supplies from Tennessee down to Sherman's forces in Georgia.

Resaca fell the morning of May 16 and Johnston ordered his armies to push west through Rome, then back east around Barnsley Gardens (along what is now I-75), and South down through the Allatoona Mountains where Sherman ultimately forced Johnston to abandon his position.

By the end of May, Northern and Southern forces were moving on Dallas and Lost Mountain, just west of Marietta. Sherman's nearly 100,000 forces were feeling the pinch of delayed supplies as Sherman holed up in Paulding County, just west of Dallas.

A Confederate soldier remarked, *"You would have breakfast with a man who was dead by lunch time."* Most soldiers referred to the fighting as "slaughters" or "bloodbaths" that had accomplished little except the taking of human life.

Joe E. Johnston maneuvered Sherman into relinquishing his hold in the Allatoona Mountains which caused Sherman's General Hooker to run head-on into Johnston's fortifications at New Hope Church. The siege lines at New Hope Church were referred to as the "Hell Hole."

Two days later, on May 27, Sherman was again surprised when Confederate troops under General Cleburne hammered Union forces at Picketts Mill. It was a battle that lasted the night through a blinding rainstorm as thunder rocked the land, and lightening pierced the darkness. When dawn filled the morning sky, 2,100 Union soldiers and 500 Confederate soldiers lay dead in the mud. Three days later, the Confederates suffered huge losses in the Dallas battle.

Sherman knew the Confederate forces would not be so easy to defeat--and right he was. His advances and Johnstons' retaliations were making the Yankees' onslaught a campaign of maneuvers and out-maneuvers as Sherman pressed on with his "horseshoe" strategy.

## June 1864

Johnston's General Leonidis Polk was killed when a cannon ball ripped through his chest, tearing off both of his arms. On June 18, Federal troops began moving east along the Dallas Highway, toward Marietta, forcing Johnston to fortify his lines of defense at Kennesaw Mountain just north of Marietta.

The Western and Atlantic Railroad in Marietta was Sherman's target. It was his strategy to break the back of the South by destroying the railroad systems.

The Rebel troops west of Marietta were a detachment to be reckoned with as the June 22 battle at Kolb's Farm proved to the advancing Yankees. Johnston's men effectively halted Sherman's attempt to bypass Kennesaw Mountain by moving directly on Marietta and attacking its North-South rail line.

Screaming and wounded Federal soldiers were suddenly caught in fires that broke out on the Cheatham Hill line not far from Kolb's Farm. A temporary ceasefire ensued as Rebel soldiers yelled to their enemies, *"Come and get your men for they're burning to death!"* Men in Confederate gray threw down their rifles, ran to the Union soldiers, and dragged them out of the raging brush fires.

Though enemy fought enemy, mercy prevailed and, in the morning, it is said that Federal commanders delivered to the ranking Confederate colonel a matching pair of ivory-handled Colt .45 pistols. Upon accepting the revolvers, the Confederate colonel said, *"I'll be glad to shoot them at you tomorrow."*

Northern General George Thomas was defeated on June 27 as he obeyed Sherman's orders for a frontal attack against the Confederate lines that encircled Kennesaw Mountain.

A solid line of Blue came again and again in their assault on the Confederate lines where the wounded, dead and dying lay at the foot of Kennesaw Mountain. Johnston managed to withdraw his forces as General McPherson moved to outflank his retreat to Smyrna, only ten miles north of Atlanta.

# July 1864

In early July, Sherman's forces moved into Roswell where they rounded up the women who worked at the textile mills and shipped them North. On July 8, another contingency of Sherman's troops crossed the Chattahoochee on the South side of Atlanta. Atlanta's population began fleeing the city.

President Jeff Davis was furious with Joe E. Johnston's failure to stand and repel the Northern advance on Atlanta. He relieved Johnston of his command on July 18. Rumor has it that Joseph E. Johnston and Jefferson Davis became enemies when they were cadets at West Point. It is said that Johnston bounced a dinner plate off Davis' head in a quarrel--not over some strategic point of war, but over a young lady. Davis was a cantankerous sort who never forgot a slight and wasted no time in sending word to Robert E. Lee that he had withdrawn Joe Johnston and put General John B. Hood in command of the Southern forces in Georgia.

(Robert E. Lee once commented that the problem which had plagued their officer corps was the question of "who ranked." Jeff Davis had ranked Joe Johnston *below* officers whom he had out-ranked while in the service of the U.S. Army. Career military officers viewed this as an insult and an offense of the highest order, and Johnston never forgot it.)

General John B. Hood had been in Longstreet's Corps at Gettysburg where he suffered an injury to his arm which hung, like dead weight at his side. The General also lost his leg (nearly clear up to his hip) at the battle of Chickamauga the year before. He was fitted with a wooden leg (carrying a spare prosthetic that could be seen slung over his saddle) and was continuously on Laudanum, an opium derivative, along with heavy doses of whiskey.

One Atlanta newspaper carried the story of Jeff Davis' action. Unfortunately, the story provided Sherman with strategic information. Having known Hood at West Point and knowing his battlefield mentality,. Sherman fully expected that General Hood's daring nature would have him launching an immediate offensive.

Hood attacked on July 20, engaging Federal troops at the Battle of Peach Tree Creek--but lost. Five hours of intense fighting ensued. Unfortunately, Hood's strategy was not nearly as effective as Joe E. Johnston's might have been had he remained in control. Johnston wanted to allow the Federals to begin crossing the creek and while their troops were split in half, the Confederates would attack in full force.

Hood's strategy was all too reminiscent of his West Point style of warfare; he ordered his troops to amass and then attack, but it proved an all-too-late plan; the Federals had already crossed the creek and taken the high ground.

Hood then ordered Hardee's corps to move in a circuitous route east of Atlanta in an attempt to attack the Federal left flank. (This bloody encounter, known as the Battle of Bald Hill, is graphically depicted at the world-famous Cyclorama, a three-dimensional diorama of the Battle of Atlanta and its environs.)

Federal forces, under General James B. McPherson, engaged Hardee's forces on July 21. Again, the Federals held the high ground after the battle at Bald Hill. On July 22, word reached Sherman that McPherson, his West Point roommate, had been killed. It has been recorded that Sherman broke down in tears, and later wrote his wife: *"I lost my right bower in McPherson."*

July 22 commenced the nearly thirty-five days of continuous artillery bombardment on the city. One of the first shells to land in Atlanta killed a father and daughter lying in their beds. Approximately ten percent of Atlanta's population had remained in the city.

Day after day the barrage rained down on Atlanta and in the evening, campfires lined the parallels where picket lines with sharpshooters killed anything that moved.

Skirmishes continued and, at approximately noon on July 28, Federal troops west of Atlanta drew one of Hood's divisions into a ferocious battle at Ezra Church where they were defeated with over 3,000 Confederates killed, out of a total of 11,000 lost souls.

## August 1864

On August 4, Federal troops tightened their encirclement around Atlanta. Hood had no plans to leave or surrender the city. With the stores of munitions at the Atlanta depot, and with the remaining Macon and Montgomery lines still open and bringing in supplies, as well as moving the wounded out of Atlanta, Hood remained confident and securely entrenched.

The skirmishes continued around the city with pickets

firing on each other from both sides of the divide. One account holds that at dusk, after the day-long fighting, when campfires dotted the landscape, a Confederate played his cornet and sang for hours into the night as Yankees called out requests for their favorite tunes, as well.

The story goes that the cornet player failed to arrive to play one evening. A cry came from a Yankee across the picket line, *"Where's the musician?"* A Confederate shouted back, *"The firing is so hot he's afraid he'll get killed."* To which the Yankee replied, *"Okay! We'll stop firing."* The Southern trumpeter commenced with his nightly concert.

On August 18, in an effort to avoid mounting another costly frontal assault, Sherman ordered out General Hugh Judson Kilpatrick with his cavalry to cut off Hood's supply lines. After destroying the railroad tracks in East Point, Palmetto and Union City, Kilpatrick's men arrived in Jonesboro.

Around August 20, a running gun battle erupted in the streets of Jonesboro. The railroad depot (located in front of what is now the Confederate Cemetery) was blown to pieces by a cannon shot from the Chicago Board of Trade Battery, a Northern unit. Splintered shafts of wooden beams and furniture, pulverized bricks, and a flurry of tickets, stamped *Jonesboro to Atlanta,* rained down on the little hamlet.

Kilpatrick's raiders destroyed not only the railroad depot but the bales of cotton and other supplies that had been stored within it. He also blew up the courthouse, and buildings that he thought had military significance.

During the raid, General Kilpatrick's men rode their horses into one frightened lady's home and proceeded to take the family Bible, the lady's calling card case with a tortoise-shelled top, and a silk flag of the unit, the Benjamin Infantry, that bore the motto: *"Strike for your homes and your altars."*.

(The tortoise shell case was later returned by a Confederate officer who had found it on the body of a dead Yankee cavalryman near Lovejoy Station. The stolen Bible was returned by a family from Marietta who had found it among the effects of another dead Federal cavalryman. The Benjamin Infantry flag is now in the custody of the Georgia State Archives.)

There is one anecdote about Jonesboro concerning a group of Yankee soldiers who camped around a large plantation just north of town. As the family hid inside the home, Union soldiers broke into the cellar and stole all the food they could find. Then they climbed the cellar stairs and entered the home, ransacking everything in sight. Though they didn't take any ear bobs or diamond rings, they did steal the owner's socks and shirts.

The next morning, the mistress of the house saw two soldiers nearby and called to them. To her surprise, she realized that she had called to two *Union* officers. Upon hearing her story, they apologized, posted a guard around her house, and promised no harm would come to the family, and even shared their food with them. The owner's daughter wrote of this incident several years later.: *"Those men were gentlemen, even though they were Yankees."*

After driving the home guardsmen and the few Confederate soldiers out of town, Kilpatrick's men set to work destroying approximately four miles of railroad track. They tore up the rails and placed the cross ties in the middle of the street where they set fire to them. Burning cinders sailed skyward, landing on the rooftops of several homes which also caught fire. The torn-up rails were piled on top of the blazing cross ties until the iron rails began to glow and soften, then they were bent around tree trunks, rendering them unusable. (The bent rails were known as *Sherman's Neckties*. Approximately twenty of these *neckties* are still stored in Jonesboro which hopes to display them one day.)

In a drawing, made by a soldier in Kilpatrick's command, the rails are burning and Kilpatrick is said to be shouting,

*"Damn the Confederacy! I'll whip them all here in Jonesboro!"* In truth, Kilpatrick's men hated him and thought him to be an arrogant little "ass" who weighed only one-hundred pounds soaking wet, and who had the morals of a pig. Their affectionate nickname for him was *Kill-Cavalry!*

After completing his destruction in Jonesboro, Kilpatrick withdrew and, on Monday, August 22, reported to Sherman that the rail lines were all destroyed on the south side. He failed to mention, however, that a brigade of Confederate cavalry, headed by the Confederate General M.H. Jackson and a few of the town's militiamen had driven him out of Jonesboro. Kilpatrick's assessment of his campaign of destruction was that the Jonesboro line would be the one to be rebuilt in what he thought would take about ten days to accomplish.

The trains were moving out of Jonesboro the next day, August 23. Even Sherman heard the trains chugging up the South line into Atlanta. His memoirs later mentioned that he had been convinced the cavalry could not--or would not--work hard enough to disable a railroad properly.

He also had tired of Hood's defiance in refusing to withdraw from the city and ordered six divisions (60,000 men) to move on the Macon and Western Railroad to once and for all sever the last rail lines from the south--which, of course, included Jonesboro.

His plan called for moving 30,000 of his men North then West, while the balance of his army moved South. As one Yankee put it, *"It was a Grand Left Wheel."*

On Thursday evening, August 25, Sherman ordered three corps to begin their silent evacuation from their positions at Utoi Creek.

On Friday evening, August 26, Howard's Army of the Tennessee pulled out of their trenches and marched all night to join alongside Thomas' Army of the Cumberland, facing south.

On Saturday, the 27th, Sherman's divisions had a hard

march moving southward from Atlanta. By Sunday, August 28, Sherman's divisions in East Point spent the night tearing up the rails and wrapping them around trees. They even set booby-traps by digging deep holes and filling them with the cross ties, brush and trees. The Yanks added loaded shells that were rigged to explode when the Confederates removed the debris to get at the cross ties.

On August 23, President Lincoln sent a confidential memorandum to members of his cabinet: *"This morning, as for some days past, it seems exceedingly probable that this administration will not be reelected."*

By mid-afternoon on August 30th, the 15th, 16th, and 17th corps of the Union Army of the Tennessee, under Howard's command, approached the Renfroe Plantation (now known as the town of Riverdale, due west of Jonesboro). The Renfroe Plantation was a major landmark and noted on every good military map of the period. The landscape was all undeveloped countryside, strange and completely unknown to the Yankees who needed guides to steer them in the right direction.

Howard's troops represented the right flank of Sherman's *grand wheel* that had been ordered to march from Fairburn eastward toward the Macon Railroad line. The troops were thirsty, in search of water and continued moving east toward the Flint River. They fell in with Kilpatrick's cavalry and forced river crossings as Confederates fired on them. The Yankees secured their high ground positions and camped along the banks of the river.

Sherman's "horseshoe" strategy would result in a rendezvous south of Atlanta, in Jonesboro; his final game plan would then be to have his forces swing northward in a full assault on Atlanta which, hopefully, would force General Hood to surrender the city.

General Hood's reconnaissance reported back to him that the Yankees had abandoned their positions around Atlanta. At first, Hood assumed they had withdrawn to Tennessee. He received another report of Yankee troops to the south, around Jonesboro, and ordered General Hardee out to halt what he decided was another Federal attempt to destroy the rail lines south of Atlanta.

Hardee was to lead 25,000 troops to the Flint River area, near the Renfroe Plantation, and wait for the cannon shot--the signal to begin his assault. Hood told Hardee, *"Just take them down there and drive them* (the Yankees) *into the Flint River... Attack with your bayonets and drive them out! As they're fleeing, shoot them in the back!"*

## The Battle of Jonesboro
## August 31 - September 1, 1864

Howard's Army of the Tennessee was only a couple of miles west of Jonesboro, on high ground--and waiting. At about three o'clock in the afternoon, the attack began as Hardee's troops moved in for their assault. Cannon fire suddenly ripped holes in the Confederate assault line. The Yankees moved their cannons and filled the gaping hole in the Rebel line. Their cannons took aim at both ends of the opening and fired.

The men of the 30th Georgia Infantry who marched out of Jonesboro in 1861 were now marching toward the blazing fire of the Union lines, *"with their faces to the enemy and their backs toward home."*

"Blackjack" Logan was reported to have said of the advancing Confederates:

*"We tore great holes in their lines. We got so close that I heard Confederate officers on horseback yelling to their men, 'Steady men! Dress (pull in) on the line...dress on the colors (the battle flag), as on parade... dress on the colors!' It was a shame they were our enemy. I was so proud of them. "*

The Federal's 31st Illinois reported that 200 of their soldiers shot over 19,000 rounds of ammunition in one hour.

One unit of Kentucky boys fell into the ditches of a Union troop who quit firing at them so they could surrender, rather than face certain death. The Confederate color bearer managed to bury the colors in the dirt rather than allow the Federals to capture it.

(The "battle flag" was the Confederate Flag bearing the cross of St. Andrew with its thirteen stars symbolizing the original thirteen colonies and what would have been the thirteen states that had seceded and joined the Confederacy. Historians have debated whether the states of Kentucky and Missouri *officially* seceded from the Union. However, the men from Kentucky and Missouri who did stand with the South were called the *Orphan Brigade*.)

Fifteen-hundred Confederates lay dead after the battle while only 150 to 250 Federals were lost; two of whom were awarded the Medal of Honor for bravery. The Yankees learned from their prisoners that Hood had only sent 25,000 Rebel forces down the rail line to Jonesboro. The Federals also learned that the Confederates had misjudged their strength, thinking the Yankee forces were only a raiding party. (A captured soldier or deserter often revealed whatever they knew about troop movements. Today, the rules of engagement are considerably different which state that soldiers are required only to give they name, rank, and serial number.)

General Hood, still at his headquarters in Atlanta, had no way of knowing what was really happening in the field... he received reports that one of the trains heading from Atlanta to Jonesboro was steaming full throttle--*in reverse*--back to Atlanta. It had been shot full of holes by Union troops moving up from the Southside.

Hood misinterpreted the Federal troop movements--again--and concluded that the Yankees were returning to Atlanta. He dispatched a rider to push through enemy lines with orders for General Hardee to withdraw half of his troops--approximately 12,000 men--and send them *back* to Atlanta.

Hood's rider took out for General Hardee with the new orders; Hardee was already withdrawing his troops from the Flint River and heading for Jonesboro where they began digging trenches along the railroad tracks, and down through the center of town. Their defense lines swept along the tracks and crossed over to and around the Federal styled white, two-story clapboarded Guy Warren House. It looked rather forlorn, perched on a knoll directly across from the rail line on the edge of town which was the "high point" in Jonesboro.

Guy Lewis Warren was the town's railroad agent; he was also a Yankee who had married Mary Vardell of Charleston, South Carolina, in October of 1838. About 1844, they moved to Jonesboro where he operated a hardware store and never failed to remind people that he sold the nails that built the majority of buildings in Atlanta.

Sometime during the first day's battle, west of Jonesboro, "Blackjack" Logan's artillery fired a cannon ball that boomed through the air, punched a hole in a second floor wall of a house, and tore a hole in a bed's headboard as a lady lay giving birth. The cannon ball thudded into the fireplace. Being a solid shot, similar to a bowling ball, it did not explode.

The family took a minute to compose themselves, then the father (future grandfather) ran outside waving a bed sheet. The artillery commander sent a rider to see what the man wanted: *"We ain't trying to take sides or get involved, but could you move the artillery to the right or to the left a little bit?"*

Upon hearing the request and reason for it, the artillery officer moved the battery down the road. According to family history, General "Blackjack" Logan presented himself at the house, along with his cavalry escort, a medical officer, and a priest.

As Logan sat on the front porch of the house, his men made coffee in the yard and teased the General that he was the godfather of the baby since it was his artillery that started the whole thing. The priest and the medical officer went upstairs and delivered the baby. The Yankees were allowed to name the child and called the little girl *Shell Anna Marvellier*, which means *"a marvelous escape from a shell"* and she was known as *Shell Annie*.

Now, before you dismiss this story, a reporter with the Atlanta Constitution interviewed Mrs. Shell Anna (Holt) Tidwell who stated:

*"My father, Tom Holt, was away fightin' when that battle (Jonesboro) was going on. I was six months old afore he saw me--that was after he was released from prison. He was captured and held prisoner for thirteen months,"* she explained, *"but he got back alright after the war was over..."*

*I reckon I had the most excitin' time gettin into the world of anybody in my family.,"* the white haired old woman surmised. *"There were twelve of us children and I'm next to the oldest... I kinda wish they had called me Marvallier,"* she interposed. *"That's a real pretty name."*

Another baby was born as the action commenced that hot August afternoon of the 31st. Mrs. E.L. Hanes, the wife of the postmaster, who was away fighting in the War, was expecting a child near any moment. She had no way of getting out of Jonesboro, except for a neighbor, W.H.L. Waldrop., who put her on a straw-filled mattress in the back of his buckboard and headed toward the old Camp Plantation on the eastern side of Jonesboro.

Sadly, Mrs. Hanes went into convulsions and died. The Confederates made a coffin for her, but an advancing line of Federals confiscated it for one of their own; another coffin was made for Mrs. Hanes. Her baby, E.L. Hanes, Jr., survived.

You may remember that Melanie Wilkes was in labor during the siege of Atlanta and, subsequently, escaped with Scarlett and Rhett in the back of a buckboard wagon with her newborn son as they headed down the old McDonough Road to Jonesboro.

Father Emeriel Bliemel, a Catholic priest with the Confederate 10th Tennessee (the Bloody Tenth), was kneeling and giving the last rights to Colonel Grace of Alabama when a Union cannonball ripped his head from his shoulders. His body and severed head were buried in the yard of R.K. Holliday's home that stood on the site of the present-day County Courthouse. (R.K. Holliday was one of Margaret Mitchell's cousins.)

Throughout the night of August 31, the Yankees worked to tear up the rail lines while the Confederates continued digging their trenches and fortifications around the Guy Warren House. As the Confederates dug in, General Hood's rider finally reached Hardee, handing him Hood's orders to remove half of his troops. Fewer than 12,000 men would be left to defend Jonesboro against the Federal onslaught moving against them from the West and North of Jonesboro.

Among those who would be returning to Atlanta were the men of the 30th Georgia Infantry who, again, left their hometown, obliged to trust their beloved homes and families to their brother soldiers.

# September 1, 1864

Sherman stood on a hill about a mile west of Jonesboro in the early morning hours of September 1. He surveyed his attack plan that called for 50,000 of his men to move east toward the Confederates' trenches and their lines of defense around a house (Guy Warren's) across from the blown-up depot and tracks.

Sherman ordered his U.S. 14th Army Corps to begin their advance to close down the north front of Jonesboro, and then connect with Howard at the railroad. The Confederates dropped their entrenching tools, grabbed their rifles, fixed bayonets, and fired a volley into the advancing Yankees.

The dense undergrowth and the intensity of the Confederates' fire, had the men of the U.S. 14th faltering and falling back. Captain L.M. Kellogg, jumped onto his horse, raced ahead of his regiment's colors, and forced his men to charge the Rebel lines. He fell with severe bullet wounds, but his men had gained a foothold.

At about four o'clock in the afternoon, Sherman's 50,000 troops began their full assault. The Confederates were spread so thin that six to twelve feet separated each man as they tried to cover the rail line.

The Union troopers never broke formation and, as one Confederate recounted: *"They marched as if on parade with their bands playing and old glory waving in the breeze. "*

There was no flinching here as generals, colonels, majors, captains, and privates all went in together across what would become the deadly field that encircled the Guy Warren House.

Great swaths of Union soldiers were cut down; the Blue Lines paused and closed ranks. *"They came as the death wave, running over us like a herd of cattle, "* wrote Sgt. John Green of the 6th Kentucky.

Those who fought said the Confederate firing was so fast and furious that whole companies of Union soldiers fell as if one man.

The men squared off, eye-to-eye, fighting hand-to-hand around the Guy Warren House. Soldiers in Blue crashed in body blows against soldiers in Gray with no time for either side to reload. They killed each other with rocks, sticks, canteens of water, even their bare hands. The color bearers of a New York regiment used their flag staffs as bludgeons until they, too, were bayoneted to death; their lifeless bodies falling into the contested trenches.

The 38th Ohio watched as their color guards at the head of their line were cut down one by one. As each next man picked up the fallen flag, he, too, fell a moment later. Then another took the flag, only to leave his death grip upon its staff and moisten its folds with his warm life's blood. The 38th Ohio suffered the highest number of casualties of any Federal regiment at Jonesboro.

Men from the Union 10th Kentucky fought to the death their neighbors, the men of the Confederate 9th Kentucky. A Union officer in the thick of the battle said, *"Never have I seen the bayonet used as it was here. "*

At the Warren House, General Davis' Federals on the right flank unslung their knapsacks, fixed their bayonets, and moved at the double-quick into the fight. Swett's Mississippi Battery and Key's Battery responded to the attack with shot and shell that cut deep into the Federal lines of young and old alike who fell as if tattered stuffed dolls.

Twenty yards away, the Confederate artillery roared their rounds as countless numbers of the 78th Illinois were cut to pieces. Colonel W.T.C. Groves fell dead at the head of the 17th New York, while Colonel Absalom Baird had two separate horses shot out from under him.

Puffs of rifle fire and cannon smoke hung suspended in the heavy summer air filled with the stench of death. Boys in Blue and Gray shouting and firing one moment, hardly felt the thud of a bullet, bayonet, or cannon ball that suddenly stole their life's breath. Long-legged steeds galloped and glided as their pointed hooves cut through the heavy smoke-ladened air sailing over bodies and muskets that also had been sent airborne.

A Michigan soldier jumped on his horse yelling, *"Follow me, me lads! Michigan forever!"* A Johnny Reb shouted back: *"The hell you say!"* and shot him dead.

Four Medals of Honor were won that day in the yard of the Guy Warren House. (In fact, the Medal of Honor was first awarded during the Civil War.)

Cannon balls rained back on the Confederate trenches as Walter Nash took a drink from his canteen then, calmly tilted it and poured the rest of the water on the fuse of a Yankee cannonball that landed at his feet.

Sherman, observing the battle from a hill west of the siege, began dancing a jig and shouting, *"By God, we're rolling them up like a sheet of paper!"*

The Guy Warren House was quickly appropriated by the Federals and used as a field hospital for the overwhelming casualties from *both* sides. Screams of wounded and dying echoed the horror in the night as their torn and bullet-riddled bodies were carried onto the already blood-soaked porch to await the scalpel--serrated edged saw--or death. Surgeons amputated so many arms and legs that they were said to have been piled to the level of the windows. And the screams filled the night; voices calling out to God and to mothers as blood ran in rivers, seeping through the cracks in the floor boards and puddling under the porch.

The battle finally ended when it became too dark to fight. The Confederates, though still holding the line they had dug near the tracks, retreated under cover of night and raced to join up with General Hardee who had pulled out and headed to Lovejoy Station, south of Jonesboro. Upon learning of the defeat in Jonesboro, General Hood ordered his Confederate forces to blow up their remaining supplies and munitions that were stored in box cars at the railway depot, then gave the order to retreat from Atlanta.

Between midnight and four o'clock in the morning of September 2, Sherman heard thundering sounds in what seemed like hundreds of explosions coming from the direction of Atlanta. At first he thought it was an engagement of Northern and Southern forces on the outskirts of the city. In fact, it was the Confederates' supplies and munitions exploding at the train yards in Atlanta.

September 2 dawned clear and turned extremely hot. Sherman marched south in hot pursuit of Hardee. Union General Slocum marched to Atlanta and entered unopposed. James Calhoun and those city councilmen who remained in Atlanta walked the debris-filled streets amongst the bombed-out buildings carrying white flags of their official surrender to the Yankees who met them at the corner of Marietta Street and Northside Drive.

On September 3, Sherman sent a short note to Lincoln stating simply, *"Atlanta is ours, and fairly won."* In the days that followed, approximately 2,500 remaining citizens were forcibly evacuated from Atlanta, under Sherman's orders. It was now a "military zone."

It had been a long and hot summer for the Confederate and Federal troops. Their two months of pitched battles exhausted men, munitions, and supplies while the outcome seemed without end.

On September 17, 1864, the London Times reported that Atlanta had fallen... because of a little battle in a little town called Jonesboro.

*"Compared with the great battles of the war, the action at Jonesborough is little more than a skirmish, yet it has been more decisive than all the fighting and bloodshed in Grant's campaign."*

President Abraham Lincoln's re-election to a second term had been a *fait accompli*--thanks to Sherman's brutal Atlanta Campaign. The fall of Atlanta not only impacted the Confederacy, resulting in General Robert E. Lee's surrender at Appomattox Courthouse in Virginia a year later, but also had altered the future of the United States.

Before Sherman began his March to the Sea, he was quoted as saying that he was *"going to make Georgia howl"* and that: *"War is cruelty. There is no use trying to reform it. The crueler it is, the sooner it will be over."*

The Civil War ended on April 9, 1865 and it has been recorded that...

Out of approximately 186,000 African-American soldiers who fought with the North, approximately 38,000 were killed.

Federal casualties totaled 664,928. Total Confederate casualties totaled 483,026 which resulted in nearly 1.2 million tragedies of War.

Federal prisoners of war, and those prisoners who died in Confederate prisons, totaled approximately 241,629. Confederate prisoners of war, and those who died in Northern prisons, totaled approximately 488,610.

In January 1863, the U.S. government estimated that the War was costing $2.5 Million per day. In 1879, a final "official" cost to the U.S. government was estimated at $6.2 Billion. The Confederacy spent $2.1 Billion fighting the War.

48 Peter Bonner

## The Townspeople And Their Stories

The Civil War -- or "The Late Unpleasantness" as the ladies of Jonesboro called it -- was a festering wound that never healed either for those who fought and survived the bloody battles, or for those whose loved ones never returned. The psychological pain of the War in the minds of Southerners, and the physical scars etched into their landscape, as the warring sides brought their battles to the homefront, were ever-constant reminders that neither they nor their successive generations could forget.

It is said that in the evening one could walk down the streets of Jonesboro and hear the "clicking" sound of knitting needles, as ladies sat on their porches knitting socks for the Confederacy. They would take their homemade socks and other clothing to the home of Colonel Johnson, the Confederate Quartermaster (also a cousin to Margaret Mitchell). He purchased the items with the limited funds he kept on hand from the Confederacy and stored them in barns at the back of his house.

According to interviews with Generals Sherman and Grant after the War, the supplies found on battlefields of every campaign, including Gettysburg in Pennsylvania, and Antietam in Maryland, could be found stamped *"Made in Atlanta"* or *"Shipped from Jonesboro."*

Colonel Allen Candler, a Jonesboro citizen, was one of the first to be wounded during the onset of the battle. He was a former history professor at the Jonesboro Academy, or Middle Georgia College as it was later named. The school provided education from primary through college level and was located on College Street, just south of the current Depot.

A shell fragment hit Colonel Candler, injuring his eye and he lay on the battlefield until nightfall on August 31st. The artillery bombardment was heard at the Camp Plantation, two miles away, as the Federals moved on the town. The Colonel was discovered by Margaret Mitchell's great-cousin, Mr. Johnson, who rode his buggy through the battlefield trying to help the wounded as best he could. Colonel Candler called out to Mr. Johnson to go to the Camp Plantation and ask Mrs. Mittie Camp to send help. She, her daughter, and their Mammy, Aunt Silla, came to the battlefield pushing a wheelbarrow and rescued Colonel Candler.

He survived, having lost his eye, and did not return to teach history in Jonesboro, but to become its mayor. He was later elected Governor of the State of Georgia and then, afterward, was appointed the Archivist for the State. (The Atlanta Airport was named in his honor and called Candler Field. His cousin, Asa, is the Candler of *Coca-Cola* fame.)

A few years ago, one of my touring guests asked me to show her the site where one of her ancestors had been killed during the first day's battle in Jonesboro. I asked, "How do you know he was killed on the first day?"

She produced a typewritten document which read:

*"Not only did I know your husband, I was next to him when he was shot down on the first day's battle of Jonesboro. In 1872, it was my honor to identify his grave and body when he was buried in the Confederate cemetery nearby. Please let me know if I can be of further assistance. Sincerely, Allen Candler, Archivist of the State of Georgia"*

I took her to the battle location which concluded the mystery of her ancestor's death.

In addition to the Guy Warren House being used as a military hospital, it also served as the Federals' headquarters because Guy Warren's New Jersey cousins, serving under General Sherman, recognized the house and asked that it be spared.

The citizens of Jonesboro did not appreciate the "good fortune" that had been bestowed upon Mr. Warren. After the War, he moved to North Carolina where his wife had inherited a plantation. He sold their Jonesboro home to W.H.L. Waldrop to "pay the taxes" on his wife's North Carolina plantation.

Mr. Waldrop immediately began repairs. Although having been a Confederate, he was appointed representative of the Freed Man's Bureau in Jonesboro which helped to find work and shelter for former slaves living in Shantytown, sleeping in ditches or alleyways. Mr. Waldrop adopted a young African-American boy named Smith, who had been a slave and had no one to care for, or raise him. According to the County court records, Mr. Waldrop swore to raise young Smith as his child and to train him in the art of farming. When the young man came of age, he changed his name to Waldrop.

As noted in Margaret Mitchell's GWTW, on page 655, paragraph 2, *"abandoned Negro children ran like frightened animals about the town until... white people... took them to raise."*

When the Warren House was purchased by the Adamson family in the 1930s, there was quite a stir about the old battlefield relic. Mr. Adamson's daughter, the late Faye Gecik, told me that during the remodeling and removal of the wallpaper, they had discovered the names and sentiments of Northern and Southern soldiers who had written on the walls after the battle in 1864. Though still in grade school, Miss Gecik remembered Margaret Mitchell attending the event, walking through the house and yard, and writing notes in a binder.

I have seen the actual pencil writings on the original walls. One missive states, *"You damn Rebels, we made you skeedaddle."* Another hurriedly states, *"Dixie forever!"* and, nearby in large block letters, appeared--*Doc Thompson, 52nd Illinois.*

(The original walls were again exposed when a home healthcare facility remodeled the Guy Warren House in 1985.)

Not all of the homes in Jonesboro were destroyed by Sherman's men. Many of the homes that survived the battle in Jonesboro were filled with the wounded from both North and South. In 1864, wounded soldiers, nurses, doctors, and chaplains were considered noncombatants and medical treatment was given without regard to lines or uniforms.

Many of the towns people assisted in those makeshift hospitals helping to relieve the suffering. Sometimes, they found themselves looking into the pain-ravaged face of a friend or local citizen who had been wounded while fighting in the battle of Jonesboro.

Remember the scene of Scarlett and Melanie assisting Dr. Meade in the hospital in Atlanta when, suddenly, they recognized Frank Kennedy?

There is one story about the Carnes' home having been

spared. As the story goes, it could have been because of a fraternal affiliation the Carnes shared with William T. Sherman who was a Mason, as was Mr. Carnes.

In 1872, seven years after the War, the State of Georgia awarded a $1,000.00 grant to exhume the bodies of Confederate soldiers who had been hastily buried in makeshift graves in the yards of homes where they had fallen in battle.

I recall reading an article written by Mrs. Ella Catherine Carnes-Romeo, who recounted the story of her great-grandfather Stephen Carnes. He was the man, together with Tom, one of his former slaves, who dis-interred and re-buried the Confederate soldiers who fell during the battles in Jonesboro.

Mr. Carnes' former slave had left Jonesboro with a Yankee captain after the battle, but returned in 1865. It is rumored that Tom asked Mr. Carnes if he could come back to work for him and live on the plantation since he was not wanted up North.

54 Peter Bonner

·P·A·R·T· ·T·W·O·

56 Peter Bonner

# The Red Clay Road
# To Tara

While dates and incidents are cut and dry to historians, we must look to the fact that Margaret Mitchell herself was only one generation removed from the War; as were all the stories, the aging Civil War veterans, and those sacred remnants that remained in her ancestors' little hometown of Jonesboro. Jonesboro, just as the rest of the South, has lived with the memories of the ravages of the War...

Born in 1900, Margaret Mitchell had the benefit of direct lineage to those who survived the War. Both her maternal grandmother and great aunts shared with little Margaret their living testimonies of the War's devastation and the deprivation that resulted.

The personal tragedies that befell the townspeople of Jonesboro are also a vital part of my *Gone With the Wind Tour* as is the actual chronology of historical events. These calamities and anecdotal stories from residents of Jonesboro's past give credence to only a part of the depth and breadth of Margaret Mitchell's own historical research and personal ancestry.

Perhaps, the one most influential incident in Margaret's

young life was the day her mother drove her to Jonesboro and pointed to the burned-out homes and the destruction that stood as daily reminders of the Civil War. Margaret Mitchell's mother impressed upon her how important it was to not only have an education, but the ability to adapt to change, and not let the past keep you down.

Margaret Mitchell was *raised on history* -- from early childhood, sitting upon *"fat, slippery laps of great aunts"* and riding horseback with her grandfather. Perhaps, a day never went by that young Margaret didn't hear how it used to be when the Yankees invaded, fought in the streets of Jonesboro, and on her great-grandfather's plantation.

*How* could Margaret Mitchell have written anything but the masterpiece that is *Gone With The Wind*?

Numerous books and commentaries have been written about Margaret Mitchell's Irish roots and their impact on and consolidation within her Pulitzer Prize winning book. Some have written that Margaret Mitchell may have been embarrassed over her Irish heritage. I believe the opposite is true.

However, one needs to understand Margaret Mitchell's Irish roots as they were planted in Clayton County, Georgia. My research has revealed that...

*"...Practically all of the incidences in the book are true.  Of course, they didn't all happen to the same person and a few of them didn't happen in Atlanta."*
Margaret Mitchell's "Gone With The Wind" Letters /  Dr. Mark Allen Patton, Virden, Illinois-July 11, 1936

---

# The Genealogy

---

## PHILIP FITZGERALD & ELEANOR McGHAN
## 1798 - 1880                    1818 - 1893

Miss Mitchell's great-grandfather, Philip Fitzgerald, born in 1798 in Legistown County, Tipperary, Ireland and was one of a family of nine who immigrated to America before 1825.  He fought in the Creek and Indian Wars and received bounty land for his services.  The North Georgia lands cleared of the Indians, attracted settlers including one of Philip's brothers who opened a general store in Fayetteville, about twenty miles southwest of what is now known as Atlanta.

Philip and a third brother helped keep the store.  Philip also  taught school, saving every cent that he earned to purchase land.

As Margaret Mitchell's brother, Stephens, wrote of his sister when she was creating the character of Gerald O'Hara:

*"He wanted to be a planter.  With the deep hunger*
*of an Irishman who has been a tenant on the lands his*

*people once had owned and hunted, he wanted to see his own acres stretching green before his eyes.   With a ruthless singleness of purpose, he desired his own house, his own plantation, his own horses, his own slaves.  And here in this new country, safe from the twin perils of the land he had left--taxation that ate up crops and barns and the ever-present threat of sudden confiscation--he intended to have them..."*

You, the reader, may draw your own conclusion as to whether Ms. Mitchell's *Gerald O'Hara* character was fashioned after her great-grandfather, Philip Fitzgerald.

Philip Fitzgerald did not start off owning slaves; however, by 1850, the county and census records showed that Fitzgerald owned 27 slaves.  The tax records for 1854 show Fitzgerald to be the owner of 2,375 acres (property then within the County of Fayette), owning 35 slaves, having a wife (Eleanor), and three daughters: Annie, Katherine, and Isabelle.

Over the next six to seven years, Philip and Eleanor had four more daughters: Adelle, Agnes Bridgett, Sarah (nicknamed Sadie/Sis), and Mary (nicknamed Mamie).  He added additional acreage to his plantation and made provisions in his Will for the Rural Home to be kept in his estate for any unmarried or widowed daughters, with their children.  Sarah and Mary never married and remained at the Rural Home until their deaths in the 1930s.

There are stories told about Philip that, in the course of his land buying, he became the owner of two parcels of land that had a farm set in the middle of the property that was being sold at auction.  He thought it a most desirable site on which to build a plantation house.

The woman, whose home it had been, stood by with her children, looked at Philip, and laid a curse on him and the land:

*"You'll never raise a man child on it,"* she said and spat at him.

Pictures I have seen of Philip Fitzgerald show a man whose stature reminds me of the Irish actor, Thomas Mitchell, who portrayed Gerald O'Hara in the movie. Stephens Mitchell referenced his sister's own description of their great-grandfather's portrait, as follows:

> *"The portrait shows him with lips firmly closed, almost grimly. There is a great deal of character and strength in his face. His eyes are hard, direct, and appraising. He had a reputation for great courage and for speaking his mind."*

A longtime resident of Jonesboro recounted an incident about Margaret Mitchell's great-grandfather, which Ms. Mitchell also mentioned. It seems Georgia Senator Hoke Smith had been going about the county making political speeches and made a stop in Jonesboro. He was addressing an issue that was neither popular nor accepted by the local people.

Senator Smith said, *"A swarm of drunken toughs"* had resented his speech, whereupon, they drew their pistols and rushed the platform, yelling: *"Let's kill him!"* Philip Fitzgerald leapt to the stage, pulled his Bowie knife from his boot, and said: *"I'll cut out the heart of anyone who touches this young man. Let him have his say!"* The drunks settled down and Mr. Fitzgerald kept a watchful eye with his knife in hand, while the nervous Mr. Smith continued his speech.

Philip Fitzgerald--*Mr. Philip,* as he was known--served as an ordinary (a judge). He also represented the County in the State Legislature at Milledgeville when it was the state capitol.

Mr. Philip's family and friends said that he would ride his horse into town *like the devil had his coattails,* when he came for court. As was the custom, the doors to the thirteen bars in underground Jonesboro, situated next to the courthouse, closed.

For those who have read Margaret Mitchell's book, she

wrote of how Gerald O'Hara left court in Jonesboro *"drunk as seven earls, jumping fences"* and singing an Irish tune.

The people of Jonesboro said that Mr. Philip would close the bars for court, reopen them, "then close them down again." When the bars finally closed at night, Mr. Philip and the other patrons would come out onto Main Street where their horses were tied.

Occasionally, the horses would get turned around and Mr. Philip would climb on his horse backwards. Patrons would yell that his horse didn't have a head. Mr. Philip responded that his horse didn't need a head, he can find his way home. He then got himself turned the right way, spurred his horse, and headed south on Main Street where it ended not far from his front door.

The Fitzgeralds, being Catholic, received the sacraments of the Catholic church only when their priest, Father O'Reilly, from Atlanta's Church of the Immaculate Conception, was able to ride the circuit to Jonesboro. When the priest arrived, the family would kneel in the parlor, hear Mass, and receive Holy Communion.

Father O'Reilly is credited with saving the churches (including his own) from General Sherman and his Union Army after the surrender of Atlanta. Upon hearing that Sherman planned to not only destroy the homes of the city's residents, but also their churches, the good Father warned Sherman that he would tell all the Irish Catholics in Sherman's army to go home--and they would! Sherman threatened to have Father O'Reilly shot, but one of his generals told him that if he shot the priest, the Irish Catholics in his army would riot, hang Sherman from a tree outside his office, and still go home! Sherman thought better of it and left the churches standing in their present locations which I am proud to include in my GWTW tour.

At the edge of Jonesboro, near a picket fence, is the headstone of a prominent planter who was killed while jumping his horse over a four-rail fence. He was doing what he loved to do best – jump horses and make friendly wagers with his long time friend and fellow fence jumper–Philip Fitzgerald. In keeping with the spirit of his favorite sport and his closest friend, the man was buried where he had fallen.

It so happens that a descendant of this gentleman came into a local drugstore where one of my part-time employees worked. The lady brought in a roll of film to be developed and upon receiving the developed pictures, showed my employee the photographs of a headstone while recounting her ancestor's death. Her ancestor was, in fact, the same friend of Philip Fitzgerald. When asked if she would allow me to share the story on my tour, she insisted that neither her ancestor's name nor the headstone's location be revealed.

(Recall, if you will, that is how Gerald O'Hara died.)

Philip Fitzgerald was 67 years old when the War ended in 1865. Having been a slave owner, he suffered tremendous financial losses, as did all the other slave-holders in the South. His slaves were free and his large plantation needed laborers to work the land. As tenacious as Mr. Philip was known to have been, he would not allow himself to be beaten and continued to work his plantation. He reestablished himself and his fortunes and died in May 1880 at the age of 82. Mr. Philip rests with his wife and other family members in a marked cemetery plot which is on my tour.

Margaret Mitchell's brother, Stephens Mitchell, described his great-grandmother, Eleanor, writing that she

*"...was very beautiful with pale gold hair, large blue eyes, and dead white skin that would not freckle. But her greatest beauty of all was her speaking voice. This was remembered by all who knew her. They called it 'silvery'"*

Stephens Mitchell added.

*"The McGhan's came to Maryland at an early date. After the Revolution, with other Catholic families, they came south to Georgia, and settled at Locust Grove."*

Despite her frailty, Eleanor birthed seven daughters, never having had a son. And, it is well known, almost as Jonesboro lore, that Eleanor Fitzgerald was a very compassionate lady who cared for those less fortunate. Perhaps, it was her Irish Catholic upbringing but everyone knew Eleanor Fitzgerald, or Miss Ellen, could be called upon whenever the need arose.

According to Stephens Mitchell's account:

*"Of all Grandmother's sisters, only Sarah and Mary did not marry. Yet Aunt Sadie (Sarah) was the beauty of the family, the one who most closely resembled her mother... She was slender, taller than Grandmother, with dark blue eyes and the prettiest yellow hair I ever saw...*

*"Her beau had been killed in the War, but no one ever heard her lament or mention this. It was said of her,* according to Margaret, *that she could rise from her seat on her back porch with a pan of snap-beans in her hand to receive the King of England or the Pope of Rome in the gracious and proper manner called for'* ... *She had the same silvery, laughing voice that drew everyone, especially children, to her."*

# ANNIE FITZGERALD & JOHN STEPHENS
# 1844 - 1934        1833 - 1896

In the seventy years since Margaret Mitchell's GWTW
was published, parallels have been drawn between Margaret's
grandmother, Annie Stephens, and that of her novel's character,
Scarlett O'Hara.

Annie Fitzgerald was educated at the Female Academy in
Fayetteville.  You will remember that in the book version of
GWTW, Margaret Mitchell wrote, *"Scarlett had not willingly
opened a book since leaving the Fayetteville Academy the year
before."* The Academy was housed for a short time in the home
of Margaret Mitchell's distant uncle in the Holliday family. The
home still stands and has been restored to its ante-bellum beauty.

Annie's two sisters, Sarah and Mary, were educated at a
convent in Charleston, South Carolina. Annie married John
Stephens (also an Irish immigrant) in 1863 in the Church of the
Immaculate Conception in Atlanta.

Family lore has referenced that John Stephens, an accountant and captain on the staff of the Commissary General in Atlanta, was Sarah's beau *before* he became interested in and, subsequently, married Annie.

> *"After she* (Annie) *married she would go back to the farm to visit her parents, taking her children with her. These were girls. She bore twelve children; lost several boys in infancy, and only her last child, a boy, survived and inherited what remained of the Fitzgerald farm,"* according to Stephens Mitchell.

The late Stephens Mitchell regarded his grandmother as having been "tough" and, as his sister, Margaret, wrote:

> *"After the battle of Jonesboro in 1864, the town was full of freed negroes, Yankee soldiers and recently paroled Confederate soldiers. The young Annie did not feel safe. She marched through the Federal camp to the headquarters of the Union general, who was probably named General Wilson, and requested a guard of Union soldiers to protect the Fitzgerald home."*

Scarlett exhibited the same gumption when she faced the Yankee deserter at Tara, the robbers in Shantytown, and her spirited trip with Mammy into postwar Atlanta when Scarlett went to visit Rhett in jail.

As best as I have been able to ascertain, Annie was just like her father, Philip Fitzgerald, to the extent of her love of the land and desire for it. While her husband, John, was off fighting in the War, Annie is said to have taken the last train out from Atlanta and went to live with one of her sisters in Macon until the end of the War, according to Stephens Mitchell. However, another account suggests that Annie left Atlanta and returned to the Rural Home where she remained, staving off starvation and fighting carpetbaggers.

It is not clear as to when Annie Stephens actually returned to the Rural Home in Clayton County.

City records, along with Jonesboro lore, hold that Annie exerted considerable influence over her husband to purchase land in the Jackson Hill area on the east side of Atlanta after the War. They became heavily invested in real estate which presented John Stephens with the opportunity to start his own trolley company to specifically serve their holdings. To my way of thinking, this illustrates the connection between Philip Fitzgerald's love of the land as Margaret Mitchell conveyed in her book through her character, Gerald O'Hara, with the words:

*"Land's the only thing in the world that matters!*
*The only thing worth working for, fighting for, and dying*
*for!. Because it's the only thing in the world that lasts!"*

A wholesale grocery business and a lumber company were located on Alabama Street in Atlanta and provided additional growth opportunities for the young couple. It is said that when John Stephens was asked how he was able to do so well after the War when others, North and South, were splitting rails? He responded, *"I guess I've always been good with numbers."*

In fact, his 1896 obituary stated that he made *"quite a fortune."* You'll remember that Margaret Mitchell's Frank Kennedy character also owned a general store *and* a lumber mill.

After John Stephens' death, Annie managed all of their properties and businesses. It has been said that her interests were far more focused on her land and business holdings than on her eight children.

68 Peter Bonner

# ISABELLE STEPHENS & EUGENE MITCHELL
## 1872 - 1919        1866 - 1944

Being the daughter of Annie Stephens, Isabelle (May Belle as her family called her)

*"loved the plantation where she had spent a lot of time in her early childhood. She was inclined to be delicate and it was thought she would thrive better there than in Atlanta in a house brimming over with children. She was Philip's (Fitzgerald) favorite grandchild and she dearly loved him and had innumerable stories to tell us about him and about the place as she remembered it. He always wanted her to sit on his knee, to ride behind him, or go with him in his buggy on visits about the county,"*
as Stephens Mitchell describes their mother.

May Belle was not nurtured by her mother as much as she was by her aunts Sadie and Mamie. It is from these aunts that she acquired her desire for book learning and education, particularly in Catholic tradition, and in art and literature.

Eugene Mitchell, the grandson of a Methodist minister, met and married Isabelle Stephens in 1892. They were living with Isabelle's mother, Annie Stephens, in 1900 when their daughter, Margaret, was born.

Eugene Mitchell was an attorney who practiced in Atlanta and who established the Mitchell law firm where his son ultimately became a practicing attorney. Eugene Mitchell was also president of the Atlanta Historical Society and an historian in his own right. There should be no doubt, therefore, that Margaret was well versed in history.

It is my personal belief that because May Belle was plagued with health problems, she must have been consumed in wanting her own daughter, Margaret, to achieve what she was unable to accomplish because of her health and, of course, the mores of society.

May Belle had a deeply Catholic sense of Christian charity toward those less fortunate, the sick and in need. It was this characteristic that ultimately made her vulnerable after caring for neighbors who were sick with the flu. This occurred while Margaret was away at the prestigious Smith College in Massachusetts in 1919.

Margaret received word that her mother was ailing but, sadly, was unable to get home before her mother passed away. Miss Ellen, Scarlett's mother, died before Scarlett could get back to Tara. Her death, the result of having cared for the less fortunate--or, the *"white trash, Emmy Slattery."*

I can only regard this literary "coincidence" as Margaret Mitchell's personally heartfelt loss--one she could not ignore. I believe she felt the need to honor her mother by encapsulating within her story not only her mother's Christian spirit, but also the issue of her mother's untimely death.

Another possible homage to Margaret Mitchell's mother is the use of her name for one of her characters, *Maybelle* Meriweather. For those who read the book or those who saw the movie, Maybelle Meriweather was the young Atlanta girl Scarlett met at the fundraising ball for the Confederacy.

The plantation Margaret Mitchell's great-grandfather owned in Jonesboro was named the *Rural Home*. Her mother, May Belle Stephens-Mitchell, often took Margaret and her brother to the country home where her two great-aunts, Mary (Mamie) and Sarah (Sis), lived and continued to maintain the home and plantation.

Margaret Mitchell was a doting and curious child. She wrote about how she had *"sat on the fat slippery laps"* of her great-aunts listening to family stories, and their recollections about the War Between the States. She was a beautiful little tomboy who rode horses, played sports, and raced over the hills that surrounded the Rural Home.

72 Peter Bonner

# Rural Home

## *Was it Tara?*

*"The Harp That Once Through Tara's Halls*
*The soul of music shed,*
*Now hangs as mute on Tara's walls,*
*As if that soul were fled.*
*So sleeps the pride of former days,*
*So glory's thrill is o'er,*
*And hearts, that once beat high for praise,*
*Now feel that pulse no more.*
*No more to chiefs and ladies bright*
*The harp of Tara swells;*
*The chord along, that breaks at night,*
*Its tale of ruin tells.*
*Thus Freedom now so seldom wakes,*
*The only throb she gives,*
*Is when some heart indignant breaks,*
*To show that still she lives."*
-- Thomas Moore, Irish Poet 1779-1852 --

The mystery continues all these seventy years since the publication of Margaret Mitchell's masterpiece and David O. Selznick's 1939 film debut of her book...

I vividly recall when people from around the world came to Atlanta to attend the 1996 Olympics. They came *expecting* to see Tara at the end of the runway. They thought they were going to drive around, hear the theme music, turn a corner--and there would be Tara! There has been many a broken heart leaving the Jonesboro depot after learning that GWTW was filmed on the back lot of Selznick's Hollywood studios. In fact, the Tara facade was later the home of the fictional Barkley family in the television series, "The Big Valley."

However the *Tara* in Margaret Mitchell's imagination still stands today, for it was the Rural Home built by her great-grandfather, Philip Fitzgerald. Miss Mitchell said, *"When I wrote GWTW, I even imagined the Fitzgerald house sitting up on a hill."*

So, let us begin with some historical facts which may have led to the fiction.

Stephens Mitchell described the Rural Home:

*"Margaret and I were very happy there. Our memories of the old place remained vivid--the land sloping away to the muddy Flint River, which 'wrapped it like a curving arm and embraced it on two sides...' In earlier days the slopes had been planted with vineyards which yielded a choice wine. Five acres were planted with apples and there was a big peach orchard..."*

He continued:

*"From Margaret's history of the family: 'The Fitzgerald house was not large, and like many farmhouses of that day, was surrounded by a ring of two-room guest houses'."*

To quote Miss Mitchell:

*"...I described it as a typical Clayton County house, 'ugly and sprawling' but comfortable looking...*

*Tara was very definitely not a white columned mansion."*

She seemed to know--perhaps, even anticipated--that Hollywood would present *Tara* in a way that would feed the public's romanticized perceptions of how people lived in the old South.

Unequivocally, there does not, nor did there, exist a house known as "Tara," nor was there a plantation that even remotely resembled the one David O. Selznick presented in his film.

William B. Hesseltine, who authored *The South and American History*, c1936, Prentice Hall History Series, states:

*"Although fiction has pictured the South as a land of great plantations, and nostalgic postwar generations have given credence to the legend, the old south was in reality a land of small farms. Except in a few localities, the plantation was comparatively rare and small holdings were the rule... Plantations varied from a few hundred to several thousand acres. The average being about 1,000 acres."*

Wilbur G. Kurtz, Atlanta's Official Historian and consultant to David O. Selznick, wrote in his letter of May 14, 1937, to Mrs. A.B. Smith of Jonesboro:

*"Don't let anyone kid you about where Tara was-- it was no existing house--it is pure fiction, but the Tara country is there and anyone can see it who cares to ride that red clay road from Lovejoy to Fayetteville. The road leaves the Dixie Highway, not at Orr's--but just before you cross the railroad going South. The Flint River Valley, as seen along that road is just what is described in the novel--excepting the item of hills West of the Flint. Twelve Oaks stood on a hill West of the Flint--but there was (not), nor is there any Twelve Oaks, and the hills are products of that faith which is said to move mountains! I saw this country with Miss Mitchell last April as did some of the movie people."*

I learned that photographers accompanied Director George Cukor and Hope Erwin, the film's original interior decorator, on a tour of the Clayton County area in mid-1937. Margaret Mitchell is said to have conducted the tour, pointing out areas and portions of territory where she had placed her fictional plantations of Tara and Twelve Oaks.

The Rural Home remained in the Fitzgerald family for years, sitting not far from the Crawford Plantation. There was a winding path that connected the two plantations. A story is told by some old timers who lived near the two plantations that John Crawford occasionally walked the path between the two estates to visit Annie Fitzgerald.

Margaret Mitchell is known to have said that her great-grandfather's Rural Home was her model for Tara. So, one might assume, as have the people of Jonesboro over the years, that the Crawford Plantation represented Margaret Mitchell's "Twelve Oaks."

In 1942, Governor Eugene Talmadge acquired the Crawford Plantation, which later became the home of his son, Senator Herman Talmadge and his wife, Betty. Sometime in the 1980's Betty Talmadge bought the Fitzgerald "Rural Home" and relocated it to her property at the Crawford-Talmadge Plantation where it sits today. Sadly, the Rural Home is in a deteriorating state.

It has been said by some that the Fitzgerald house had green velvet portieres (drapes) in the parlor. Thus far, I haven't found any corroborating data to confirm this. However, it is known that the Crawford ladies in 1864 took down their drapes and made them into new dresses. So today, within 100 yards of each other, stand the green velvet drapes-to-dresses historical account, and the drapes-to-dresses story in fiction.

Inevitably, during my tours someone will ask about the shooting of the Yankee soldier at the foot of the staircase. *"You*

*Yankees have been here before..."* Scarlett told the marauding Federal soldier at the foot of the staircase at Tara.

My response is always a definitive "I can't confirm whether that incident actually happened in Jonesboro." There have been many in town who claim to have seen "stains" at the bottom of the staircase in the Fitzgerald Rural Home, however, there is no substantiation of this allegation.

Margaret Mitchell referred to the shooting of a Yankee deserter; however, she recalled that it probably came from a story she found about General Wilson's raid in Alabama. She explained that there were a number of break-ins by Union soldiers, very much like the one she wrote about in her book.

I have read several accounts that Union troops had camped at the Fitzgerald Rural Home around the time of the battles of Jonesboro. They destroyed somewhere in the neighborhood of $50-60,000 worth of cotton; in addition to livestock, produce, and other property.

A period of "Reconstruction" followed the Civil War. I was told that five southerners could not meet together without a Federal Marshall present. The Union soldiers, now victors, wanted to go home. They didn't want to stay and police, or sheriff the south.

The men of Jonesboro met in secret in order to create committees to discuss rebuilding their town. In fact, because of rioting by former slaves and displaced persons, the leaders of the town took to riding through Jonesboro at dusk, four abreast, from one end of the city to the other--the signal that people should get off the streets--oftentimes associated with the Ku Klux Klan.

Many will remember the *secret political meetings* – like the one Ashley Wilkes and Frank Kennedy attended... the night Ashley returned home with a bullet in his shoulder, and Rhett Butler apologized for bringing the men to Belle Watling's...

The period of Reconstruction ended for the people of Georgia in 1870 when the state was formally readmitted to the Union. The peoples' lives under Federal occupation was not forgotten. Plans for the new school superintendent's house included a "secret room" with a passageway for escape. They also constructed a tunnel under the house. As it turned out, it was not a tunnel but a bomb shelter, built at the same time as the house. If the country went back to war with the Yankees *after* 1879, plans were to move the court records down into the bomb shelter safe from the fighting.

# MATTIE HOLLIDAY

*"...you know the Wilkes always marry their cousins,"* Margaret Mitchell wrote of Melanie Hamilton Wilkes in *Gone With The Wind.*

Here is a little genealogy for you...

James Fitzgerald (one of Philip Fitzgerald's brothers) married Mary Anne O'Carew. They had a daughter, named Mollie who married Robert Kennedy Holliday--and they had a daughter, named Martha Anne (Mattie) who was born in 1848 (died in 1939).

Mattie Holliday's father, Robert *Kennedy* Holliday, marched off to war in 1861, but was captured at Gettysburg, and disappeared thereafter. At the end of the war, Mattie and her family returned to live at the Fitzgerald's Rural Home.

As noted previously, the Union Army destroyed R.K. Holliday's residence after the battle of Jonesboro. Years later, Mattie Holliday stated that the Yankees had desecrated her family's home by holding a drunken party with loose women, and then, tore it down and used the debris for fire wood. To make matters worse, Mattie would forever live with the thought that Father Bliemel's decapitated body had been buried in their front yard.

(The Courthouse, built around the turn-of-the-century, stands on the site of the former Holliday home.)

I learned from many of the towns folk that they had seen Margaret Mitchell walking the grounds where R.K. Holliday's home had stood, as well as spending many hours in the Courthouse doing research. According to a newspaper article I found in the Jonesboro archives:

> "A petite dark haired woman came into the office of Superior Court Clerk P.K. Dixon one day in the early 1930s and asked if she could check some of the court records for a book she was writing... She said she had almost finished her book, and the publishers were anxious to have it, recalled Dixon...."

One afternoon, while the folks at Rural Home were feeding the ragged Confederate soldiers who had returned from the War, another scarecrow in a tattered Rebel uniform came walking down the dirt road toward the house. The closer he came, the family realized it was Robert Kennedy Holliday coming home. (Shortly after his return, a photo was taken of him in his Confederate uniform that clearly shows the protruding ribs on his 6-foot frame.)

After the war, Robert *Kennedy* Holliday attempted to rebuild his mercantile store, but did not live long enough to realize his dream. His daughter, Mattie, had "no use" for the Yankees and said that her father's death was as a result of having been a prisoner of war after fighting at the Battle of Gettysburg.

It should be noted that Robert Kennedy Holliday's store still stands in Jonesboro today. However, it wasn't until a few years ago when it was learned that his store had survived the

Battles of Jonesboro. The current owner of Holliday's store discovered its identity during a title search prior to the real estate closing on the property. It was listed as having been R.K. Holliday's office building in 1850. Upon learning this information, along with finding an original photograph (on glass), the owners contacted me. I identified the photo as Mattie Holliday's mother.

OKAY, now...

Mattie Holliday was in love with John Henry Holliday, a Presbyterian *and* her first cousin. The problem was not that John Henry was a Presbyterian and she a Catholic, but that the Catholic Church did not (and still does not) permit first cousins to marry.

John Henry Holliday was born in Griffin, Georgia, but the family relocated to Valdosta to avoid the War in 1861. Mattie and her mother left Jonesboro at about the same time and went to stay with the Hollidays in Valdosta and did not return until after the War.

Some time during the mid- to late 1860s, Mattie entered a convent in Savannah and John Henry went to dentistry school in Philadelphia. He graduated in 1872, returned to Atlanta to open a practice, then relocated his practice to Griffin where he had inherited an office building. Upon learning that he had Tuberculosis, he moved West. He had been a rather sickly young man, about five-foot-seven-inches tall, and weighed about one-hundred-fifteen pounds.

Mattie resolved her love for John Henry by taking her vows as a *bride of Christ* and becoming a nun with the Sisters of Mercy in 1873. She took the name Sister Mary *Melanie*, and was known as Sister *Melly*.

Stay with me...

History has recorded that the man Sister Melly loved, John Henry Holliday, became a dentist and moved west because of bad health. He is known in the history books as John Henry

*"Doc"* Holliday, the "deadly" dentist gambler who joined Wyatt Earp and his brothers in the famous shoot-out at the OK Corral in Tombstone, Arizona.

In the movie, *"Tombstone"* with Val Kilmer (Doc Holliday) and Kurt Russell (Wyatt Earp), Doc says to Wyatt as he lay dying of consumption, *"There was only one person I ever wanted, my cousin, and I couldn't have her."*

Upon his death, Doc Holliday's trunk of personal effects was shipped to Sister Melly. In his trunk were all of her letters that he had kept down through the years.

As a retired Mother Superior in Atlanta during the 1930s, Sister Melly was visited by her cousin, Margaret Mitchell, who asked, *"May I use you in my book?"*

Sister Melly responded, *"If you're going to use me, make me somebody nice."*

No one has ever regarded Margaret Mitchell's Melanie Hamilton character as anything but a truly sweet and "nice" person. It was a promise Margaret Mitchell kept to her cousin, Sister Melly. Was it Margaret Mitchell's intention to contrast the characters of "Melanie," her cousin, with that of Scarlett, (her grandmother)?

Family and friends and all who knew Sister Melly said, *"She was the kindest woman we ever knew."* Margaret Mitchell's Rhett Butler said of Melanie Hamilton following her death: *"She was the only completely kind person I ever knew... She was a very great lady."*

Personally, I don't believe anyone could have portrayed Melanie Hamilton with the depth of gentility as Olivia de Havilland did. She, too, is a *very great lady.*

Sister Mary Michael, RSM, of St. Joseph's Infirmary in Atlanta, wrote to Mrs. Susan McKey Thomas of Valdosta, Georgia in 1972:

"I know Margaret Mitchell must have been devoted to Sister, or she would not have made the lovely character in the story be named Melanie, after Sister Melanie.

"I lived with Sister Melanie in Augusta around 1928. She talked much about her brother 'Jim-Bob' and about his children, but I really cannot remember, as I was then quite young, and not too long from Ireland. She certainly had 'no use for the Yanks,' and she did not hesitate to tell us that."

# The Characters

## RHETT BUTLER

He needs no introduction. He stands tall as a ladies' man, yet a true man's man--dashing and daring in every way possible. Clark Gable personified the character of Rhett Butler as, perhaps, no other Hollywood actor could have.

Down through the last seventy years and the countless millions who have read Margaret Mitchell's classic, a nagging curiosity inevitably invades the readers' minds:

*Could Margaret Mitchell have known a man like Rhett Butler?*

Civil War history has documented that there was a ship's captain named Butler; unfortunately, little is known about him.

There was, however, a George Trenholm who, with John Fraser, owned Fraser, Trenholm & Company that was based in *Charleston, South Carolina.* The company was established the year before the War broke out, and is well documented to have been a major blockade running operation. It is also said that

George Trenholm was handsome and brave and worth millions by the end of the War.

Whether Margaret Mitchell based her Rhett Butler on the daring exploits of George Trenholm, we can't say with any degree of certainty. Ms. Mitchell's repeated references to her many years of intensive Civil War research would certainly open up the possibility that her fact-finding probably uncovered the Trenholm blockading exploits.

Or, did Miss Mitchell fashion Rhett Butler after the rough and wicked side of her first husband, Berrien "Red" Upshaw? For those Margaret Mitchell/GWTW devotees, the record reflects that Margaret Mitchell's marriage lasted only two years, having divorced him in 1924 after a rather stormy union. Local lore has it that Upshaw made assertions that Margaret Mitchell had based her Rhett Butler character on *him*. She denied any such allegation and nothing more came of it.

# PRISSY

Margaret Mitchell is known to have said, *"Prissy was a real person."*

During my early years of touring visitors around Jonesboro, I shared the story about a local planter, Sherod Gay. He had created a dowry for his daughter who was engaged to marry a Confederate officer in 1861. The dowry consisted of 500 acres, a house, several barns, and one slave, named Prissy.

I was fortunate to have uncovered the 1870 census records for Jonesboro in Clayton County. The entry reads:

*"Prissy Gay, age 52, female, black, keeping house at number 108."*

Also listed among the slaves in the household with Prissy, is a male servant, named *Pork*, or *Polk*. (It is difficult to discern the illegible handwriting.)

Doing the math, Prissy would have been born in 1818 and been approximately 43 years old in 1861, when she was given to Mr. Gay's daughter and new son-in-law. She lived with the young couple in the Jonesboro area until the end of the War, then moved into the city limits.

A City Directory for Jonesboro lists a black gentleman, named *Uncle Peter* McElroy, doing business as a hack (buggy driver). You'll remember Aunt Pitty-Pat's carriage driver was named *Uncle Peter*.

# MAMMY

Margaret Mitchell's *Mammy* may not be the personification of one living person. I believe it is the "character" of a Mammy in those times and that Ms. Mitchell's *Mammy* was more a compilation of a number of "Nanny" caregivers who lived in Jonesboro during the War Between the States.

As a storyteller, verbally recounting the history I personally research, I have found it not only essential but critical to understand the *personalities* of those I am recalling.

I learned that a black servant 144 years ago so loved her "masters" that she requested to be buried in their family plot... And when I learned that her masters willingly allowed such a burial request, I had to conclude that there *must have been* a greater bond, perhaps, a *loving* bond of slave for master, and of master for slave.

This unique and often misunderstood relationship has

been presented throughout fiction and the entertainment media, in my opinion, in a multitude of unfair portrayals. There were two distinct classes of slaves; the house workers and those who tended the fields. Recalling Margaret Mitchell's portrayal of Mammy, Pork, Prissy; and Big Sam (one of the O'Hara field hands), Scarlett made no distinction between her respect for, or dependency upon, the O'Hara slaves.

Conversely, all the local stories about the slaves who lived in and around Jonesboro... such as Tom, "the colored man," who returned to Jonesboro after the War and asked his former owner, Mr. Carnes, to give him back his job... And,

Aunt Silla who lived on the Camp Plantation and who risked her life to help her mistress, Mrs. Mittie Camp, rescue Colonel Allen Candler after the Battle of Jonesboro. Aunt Silla went on to raise another generation of children on the Camp Plantation following the war.

At the time the Confederate Cemetery was dedicated in Jonesboro, Colonel Allen Candler was the keynote speaker to give the official welcome and dedication of the cemetery. He deferred to another to tell the story of his rescue from the battlefield--Aunt Silla, the Mammy of the Camp Plantation.

Aunt Lucy was another beloved Mammy in Jonesboro who stood her ground* when the Yankees broke into her plantation home and ransacked the house...

Aunt Francis, yet another loving Mammy, tended to the needs of wounded soldiers--North and South--following the Battle of Jonesboro. She boiled their clothes in a huge iron washtub that sat out behind the family house. However, there is no record that Aunt Francis, like Mammy in GWTW, had dealt with the *"crawling lice and dysentery"* that plagued the returning soldiers.

An interesting aside concerning Aunt Francis... The story about Aunt Francis and the washtub originated with the owner of the old house whose grandmother was ten years old at the time of the Battle of Jonesboro. She was an eyewitness to the fighting that took place in her own front yard. Of all her recollections, the most memorable one she held was telling of the summer afternoon when Margaret Mitchell sat on her front porch and listened to all her stories about the past.

The owner of the house also explained why her home had such an "interesting" look. A fire had started on the top floor of the two-story ante-bellum structure. Her ancestors did not have the funds to rebuild the house so, he chose to "cap it off," designing it as a one-story. Over the years of stopping at that modified ante-bellum home, my touring guests rarely fail to remind me of the description Margaret Mitchell gives of Melanie and Ashley's home in Atlanta which was a former two-story house that had suffered the same fate.

And finally, at the feet of Philip and Eleanor Fitzgerald's graves, is a small headstone with the inscription, *"Grace, Negro servant of the Fitzgeralds."* Little is known about Aunt Grace, other than she was buried--at her own request--in the Fitzgeralds' family plot. I interpret this to mean that Grace was honored as a family member.

In all deference to Margaret Mitchell, although the slaves she characterized did stay with the O'Hara family after the Civil War, she does *not* say or even suggest that all slaves were happy to be slaves, nor that they all stayed on at their plantations after the War ended. As an historian, I wholeheartedly concur.

## A Closing Word

*Gone With The Wind* has endured these long seventy years, along with the generational and moral shifts in society. It has long outlived the history books which fixate not so much on the history of that era, as they do on the relationship between free man and slave.

The millions who have read Margaret Mitchell's *Gone With The Wind* since its release in June 1936 have hitched their fantasies and their perceptions to a world and a way of life that is no more. Is it because of the breadth and depth of gentility and the compassion of her characters--black and white--that so drastically contrasts those who have lived in subsequent generations?

Or...

Is it, as Margaret Mitchell wrote, "*...about the people in the South during those hard times who had gumption and the people who didn't, and the strong will to survive.*" ?

The irony, my dear touring readers, is that while Margaret Mitchell wrote--and even made a point of clarifying--that her book was about those with "gumption" and those who were "strong willed," it is, in my humble opinion, the character of Melanie Hamilton--not Scarlett--who Margaret Mitchell ultimately chose to esteem.

Scarlett was the beautiful one. Scarlett was the strong-willed one. Scarlett was forever striving and conniving for wealth and power... perhaps like her grandmother, perhaps not...

Melanie was the loyal and dedicated one. Melanie was the persevering one, though shy and retiring, whose self-denial and consummate love showed the quintessence of the patrician world that she and Ashley knew and loved, but which dissolved before their eyes.

Rhett Butler said it best: *"Well, God rest her... She was the only completely kind person I ever knew... a very great lady."*

> *"...So sleeps the pride of former days,*
> *So glory's thrill is o'er,*
> *And hearts, that once beat high for praise,*
> *Now feel that pulse no more..."*
> -Thomas Moore, Irish Poet-

For those of you who have not yet read *Gone With The Wind*, I urge you to step back in time by reading Margaret Mitchell's all-time classic.

Thank you, my touring readers, for allowing me to share how deeply *Lost in Yesterday* I am, and for commemorating Margaret Mitchell's own love of history, along with her memories of that patrician world that, too, is forever *Gone With The Wind...*

*To Be Continued...*

# Atlanta - The Aftermath

The following is a letter, dated December 7th, 1864, Atlanta, Georgia. It is from the University of Georgia archives:

*To His Excellency Joseph E. Brown, Governor of Georgia:*

*In obedience to orders of Nov. 25, to inspect the State property in Atlanta, and the city itself, and protect the same, I have the honor to make the following report. With it I beg leave to present your Excellency with a pencilled map of the city, showing the position of every house left unburned.*

*The property of the State was destroyed by fire, yet a vast deal of valuable material remains in the ruins. Three-fourths of the bricks are good and will be suitable for rebuilding if placed under shelter before freezing weather. There is a quantity of brass in the journals of burned cars and in the ruins of the various machinery of the extensive railroad shops; also, a valuable amount of copper from the guttering of the State depot, the flue pipes of destroyed engines, stop cocks of machinery, etc. The car wheels that were uninjured by fire were rendered useless by breaking the flanges. In short, every species of machinery that was not destroyed by fire was most ingeniously broken and made worthless in its original form — the large steam boilers, the switches, the frogs, etc. Nothing has escaped. The fire engines, except Tallulah No. 3, were sent North. Tallulah has been overhauled and a new fire company organized. Nos. 1 and 2 fire engine houses were saved. All the city pumps were destroyed, except one on Marietta Street. The car shed, the depots, machine shops, foundries, rolling mills, merchant mills, arsenals, laboratory, armory, etc., were all burned.*

*In the angle between hunter Street, commencing at the City hall, running east, and McDonough Street, running southern, all houses were destroyed. The jail and calaboose were burned. All business houses, except those on Alabama Street, commencing with the Gate City Hotel, running east to Loyd Street, were burned. All the hotels, except the Gate City were burned. By referring to my map, you will find about 400 houses standing. The scale of the map is 400 feet to one inch. Taking the car-shed for the center, describe a circle, the diameter of which is twelve inches, and you will perceive that the circle contains about 300 squares. Then, at a low estimate, allow three houses to every 400 feet, and we will have 3600 houses in the circle. Subtract the number of houses indicated on the map, as standing, and you will see by this estimate, the enemy have destroyed 3200 houses. Refer to the exterior of the circle, and you will discover that it is more than half a mile to the city limits, in every direction, which was thickly populated, say nothing of the houses beyond, and you will see that the enemy have destroyed from four to five thousand houses. Two-thirds of the shade trees in the Park and city, and of the timber in the suburbs have been destroyed. The suburbs present to the eye one vast, naked, ruined, deserted camp. The Masonic Hall is not burned, though the corner-stone is badly scarred by some thief, who would have robbed it of its treasure, but for the timely interference of some mystic brother.*

*The City Hall is damaged but not burned. The Second Baptist, Second [Central] Presbyterian, Trinity and Catholic churches and all the residences adjacent between Mitchell and Peters streets, running south of east, and Loyd and Washington streets running south of west, are safe, all attributable to Father O'Reilly, who refused to give up his parsonage to Yankee officers, who were looking out for fine houses for quarters, and there being a large number of Catholics in the Yankee army, who volunteered to protect their Church and Parsonage, and would not allow any homes adjacent to be fired that would endanger them. As a proof of their attachment to their Church and love for Father O'Reilly, a soldier who attempted to fire Col. Calhoun's house, the burning of which would have endangered the whole block was shot and killed, and his grave is now marked. So to Father O'Reilly the country is indebted for the protection of the City Hall, Churches, etc.*

*Dr. Quintard's, Protestant Methodist, the Christian, and African churches were destroyed. All other churches were saved. The Medical College was saved by Dr. D'Alvigny who was left in charge of our wounded. The Female College was torn down for the purpose of obtaining the brick with which to construct winter quarters. All institutions of learning were destroyed. The African church was used as an academy for educating negroes. Roderick Badger, a negro Dentist, and his brother, Bob Badger, a train-hand on the West Point and La Grange Railroad, both well known to the citizens of Atlanta, were assistant professors to three philanthropic Northmen in this institution. Very few negroes remained in the city. Thirteen 32-pound rifle cannon, with cascabels and trunnions broken off and jammed in the muzzles, remain near the Ga. R.R. shop. One well reported to be filled with ammunition. Fragments of wagons, wheels, axles,* bodies, etc., are strewn over the city. Could I have arrived ten days earlier, with a guard of 100 men, I could have saved the State and city a million dollars.

There are about 250 wagons in the city on my arrival, loading with pilfered plunder; pianoes, mirrors, furniture of all kinds, iron, hides without number, and an incalculable amount of other things, very valuable at the present time. This exportation of stolen property have been going on ever since the place had been abandoned by the enemy. Bushwhackers, robbers and deserters, and citizens from the surrounding country for a distance of fifty miles have been engaged in this dirty work.

Many of the finest houses, mysteriously left unburned, are filled with the finest furniture, carpets, pianoes, mirrors, etc., and occupied by parties who six months ago lived in humble style. About fifty families remained during the occupancy of the city by the enemy, and about the same number have returned since its abandonment. From two to three thousand dead carcasses of animals remain in the city limits.

Horses were turned loose in the cemetery to graze upon the grass and shrubbery. The ornaments of graves, such as marble lambs, miniature statuary, souvenirs of departed little ones are broke and scattered abroad. The crowning act of all their wickedness and villiany was committed by our ungodly for in removing the dead from the vaults in the cemetery, and robbing the coffins of the silver name plates and tipping, and depositing their own dead in the vaults.

I have the honor to be, Respectfully,
Your obedient Servant,
W.P. Howard

## ·R·E·C·O·M·M·E·N·D·E·D· ·R·E·A·D·I·N·G·

❑ Mitchell, Margaret. Gone With the Wind. 1st ed. New York: The Macmillan Company, 1936.

❑ Pyron, Darden Ashbury. Southern Daughter: The Life of Margaret Mitchell. Oxford University Press U.S.A., 1991

❑ Bailey, Anne J., and Walter J. Fraser, Jr. Portraits of Conflict: A Photographic History of Georgia In the Civil War. 1st ed. Fayetteville: The University of Arkansas Press, 1996.

❑ Davis, Burke. Sherman's March. 1st ed. New York: Vintage Books, 1980.

❑ Ellingson, Paul, ed. Confederate Flags in the Georgia State Capitol Collection. 1st ed. Atlanta: Georgia Office of Secretary of State, 1994.

❑ Garrison, Webb. Atlanta and the War. 1st ed. Nashville: Rutledge Hill Press, 1995.

❑ Harwell, Richard, ed. Margaret Mitchell's "Gone With the Wind" Letters 1936-1949. 1st ed. New York: Macmillan Publishing Co., Inc., 1976.

❑ Rose, Michael. Atlanta A Portrait of the Civil War. 1st ed. Charleston: Arcadia Publishing, 1999.

❑ Strayer, Larry M., and Richard A. Baumgartner, ed. Echoes of Battle The Atlanta Campaign. 2nd ed. Huntington: Blue Acron Press, 1991.

❑ Traywick, Ben T. John Henry (The "Doc" Holliday Story). 1st ed. Los Angeles: We Print It, Inc., 1996.

❑ Watkins, Sam R. "Co. Aytch" A Side Show of the Big Show. Bell Irvin Wiley ed. Wilmington: Broadfoot Publishing Company, 1987.

❑ Scaife, William R. The Campaign for Atlanta. William R. Scaife, Atlanta, GA 1995

## *Tell us what you think about Peter Bonner's book!*

1.      <u>I bought Peter's book because:</u>
   - ❏ the cover intrigued me
   - ❏ I heard Peter Bonner on a radio/tv talk show
   - ❏ I like reading about the Civil War / Gone With The Wind

2.      <u>I think Peter Bonner's book is:</u>
   - ❏ intriguing and different than other books I've read about history
   - ❏ powerful--I couldn't put the book down
   - ❏ sensitive and compelling

3.      <u>The book made me:</u>
   - ❏ understand so much more about the Civil War
   - ❏ understand so much more about the South and Southerners

4.      <u>The book should:</u>
   - ❏ never have been written
   - ❏ be read by adults and youth alike to better understand our history
   - ❏ be available in audio version so I can hear Peter Bonner

5.      <u>I want to know:</u>
   - ❏ when Peter Bonner's next book is coming out
   - ❏ when Peter Bonner will be talking about his book or lecturing
   - ❏ when his book will be available on audiocassette or CD

6.      <u>I will:</u>
   - ❏ tell my friends to buy Peter's book
   - ❏ ask my library to order Peter's book
   - ❏ ask my local radio/tv talk show to interview Peter Bonner

NAME_____

ADDRESS_____

CITY_____STATE____ZIP_____

EMAIL_____
   - ❏ Please put my name on FirstWorks' mailing list
   - ❏ Send me ____ autographed copies of *Lost in Yesterday* @
     $15.00 each  Plus $4.50 S/H (GA residents add 6% sales tax)
   - ❏ Check is enclosed (*please allow 3-4 weeks for delivery*)
   - ❏ Money Order is enclosed (*shipped within 48 hours*)

*Make Check/M.O. Payable to:*
FirstWorks Publishing Co., Inc.
PO Box 93
Marietta, GA 30061-0093

# *firstWorks' Current Titles*

·STEPPING ON MEMORIES
by Marge Griffin-Glausier

THE PALE HORSE COMETH
by Dani Dubre' & Rod Mauck

SUGAR IN THE GOURD
by Ben Garrison

INTO THE TWILIGHT
by S.W. Lowery

## *Upcoming Titles:*

WHORE OF MADNESS
by Dani Dubre'

104  Peter Bonner

Printed in the United States
221670BV00001B/5/A

9 780971 615892